T0145164

MY MOMMY'S NOT A PEANUT!

Written by
Khristine Griffin

Illustrated by
Kelsey McSweeney

Copyright © 2017 by Khristine Griffin. 771019
Library of Congress Control Number: 2017918104

ISBN: Softcover   978-1-5434-6839-7
        Hardcover   978-1-5434-6840-3
        EBook   978-1-5434-6838-0

This is a work of fiction. Names, characters,
places and incidents either are the product of the
author's imagination or are used fictitiously, and any
resemblance to any actual persons, living or dead,
events, or locales is entirely coincidental.

Print information available on the last page

Rev. date: 02/21/2018

To order additional copies of this book, contact:
Xlibris
1-888-795-4274
www.Xlibris.com
Orders@Xlibris.com

Hi, my name is Gianna.

I think. I've heard Gianna my ENTIRE
life. But then...

The other day I was at my grandma's house and she said "come play with me PJ". My grandma always calls me PJ.

PJ??? Who is PJ? I thought my name was Gianna. But my grandma knows me so maybe my name is PJ.

.....then, I was at the store with my daddy and big people came up to me and grabbed my cheeks and said "aren't you a sweetie" and my daddy said "say thank you Gianna Pianna"

Gianna Pianna??? No, no, no, my name is PJ. But this is my daddy. So maybe my name is Gianna Pianna. I'm so confused.

...then, I was at the park with my Mammers and she yelled "GO GIGI GO" as I was sliding down the big slide.

Gigi??? But I thought my name was
Gianna Pianna? What is happening?

...then, I was at my Papa's house and I ran up to him super fast because I'm super fast and he picked me up and said "wooow Nana".

Nana??? MY NAME IS GIGI.

...then, my mommy said, "come and brush your teeth Boo Boo and get ready for bed".

Boo Boo??? But I thought my name was Nana.

That's it! This is my mommy. MY
MOMMY! She knows everything.

She has to know what my name is, I remember her from the very beginning. So My name MUST be Boo Boo.

But could I have had it all wrong? Could my name be something else? Am I not who I think I am?

And then...today, my grandma walked into the house, set her purse on the table, leaned over and gave my mommy a hug and a kiss and said "Hi, Peanut". I thought, why does she always call my mommy peanut, my mommy's not a peanut my mommy's a mommy?

AND I GOT IT!!! My mommy's not a peanut but sometimes people call her different names too and she's ALWAYS my mommy. Grandma told me it's called a nickname.

So, I'm always Gianna....but sometimes I'm PJ and sometimes I'm Gianna Pianna and sometimes I'm Gigi and sometimes I'm Nana and sometimes I'm Boo Boo but I'm always Gianna.

Hi, my name is Gianna PJ Gianna Pianna Gigi Nana Boo Boo. What's yours?